Acknowledgements

I want to give honor to God for blessing me with the ability to express in poetry what He wants me to convey so that He gets the glory and honor out of it.

Dedication

I dedicate this book of poetry to everyone who has or is experiencing any of the situations discussed in it.

To God be all the Glory!

The Love Between A Man and A Woman

The Love between a man and a woman can't be measured with words or material things.

True Love comes from action, whether it is in a hug, kiss, massage, caress, or even quality time spent with the one you love and communicating in some way form or fashion.

When a woman loves, it is unconditional; no force on earth can keep her from turning her back on the one she has committed or pledged her heart too.

The only way to overcome it is to allow God to come in and take total control.

A woman will go the distance to show the one she loves how much she truly cares and believes in him. Her faith will not only be for herself but she believes for him beyond measure. She will begin to see him being further than what he sees and will begin to speak those things unaware to the loved one. As she sees him moving into the things that have been spoken she will not say a word but will praise God for blessing the man she loves so. A woman will find herself creating ways that will ease the stress of the man she loves. All the while praying that he realizes that she really does love him beyond what eyes can see.

Ladies if you have a man that you love beyond measure and are faithful don't stop being who you are and gentlemen if there is a lady in your life that is showing all of these qualities whatever you do don't let her go, because God may never give you the opportunity to encounter a woman of this magnitude again.

Given by God; Written By:

Corrine Hooks

How Do You Let Go?

How do you let go of something or someone you have poured your heart and soul into?
It's simple you can't; that is you can't do it alone! You can only do it with the help of God. He is the only true one who can bring you through any trial, test or storm.
If you find yourself slipping away from something or someone just fall on your knees and talk to God about it because He knows all, sees all, and created all. He knows how much we can bear, and will not put more on us than we can not handle.
But if God does not tell you to let go, you better hold on as tight as you can and fight until the end because if He brought you to it, you can rest assured He will bring you through it!!!!!!!!!!
Given by God; Written by:
Corrine Hooks

There Is Nothing A Woman Can Do

There is nothing a woman can do for me that I can't do for myself. But a man, a man on the other hand, he is strong in mind, body, and soul. A man is goal-oriented and when his mind is set on doing something there is nothing he won't try or do to accomplish it. A man that is lead by God and being used by God can do anything and everything. A man that is obedient to the will of God, he will not waiver in his faith.

When that man has searched out the woman he seeks to marry and spend the rest of his life with he will go the distance to make her the queen of his castle. And that is who God has ordained for me.

Given by God; Written by:
Corrine Hooks

Love Spoken

Love can be spoken in many ways. Love can be shared by anyone!
Love is the greatest gift one can give.
God gave His greatest love which was Jesus.
Jesus gave His love by dying on the cross for us.
We are blessed to be able to give out to others the love that God, the Father, and His Son Jesus so freely give to us daily.
To share that love with someone else is infinite.
Love is a constant thing. It does not come and go.
It is first given and then received.
Love with all your heart and soul.
Given by God; Written by:
Corrine Hooks

Why Is It So Hard For Men To Believe

Why is it so hard for men to believe that God really created a woman for them? God created a woman for every man. He didn't just create woman to fit any man. There is a woman that is specifically created to be with a specific man. Just like with Queen Esther, she did not become Queen just for the Jews; she became Queen for the King as well. God ordained it that way, the same way He ordained us for the one we are to be with. Every woman has unique qualities that fit with the man God has for her. Don't count it strange if that woman does things for you that you are not use to. God has chosen her just for you because He knows your spirit since He has given it to you. She has been given to you not just for the natural man but for the spiritual man as well. She is there to feed every natural area as well as every spiritual area. She will build you up, hold you up, back you up, and fill you up with whatever God tells her to do (if she is lead of God). God did not create woman to harm man and what I mean by that is that she is not there to hurt you mentally, physically, financially, emotionally, and especially not spiritually. Ladies & Gentlemen, pray without ceasing and God will do the manifesting.

Given by God;

Written by:

Corrine Hooks

Love: Who Is It For?

Love, is it for fools or for everyone? I heard it said that you can't help who you love. Sometimes I wonder how true that is. There are people placed in our lives to bless us with a word, financial deed, or some other form of need. Are we to love them? YES! But there is one that God may place in your life that you are to love with all your heart. And that person may not realize what may have been sparked in your spirit. And sometimes it is not easy to explain with words. It is even hard to express in actions as well because what you do for them & to them; it seems that you have not gotten your point across. Are we to continue to do our best in showing them that we really do Love them? Of course!!!!!!! You know why because God knows that the man or woman is supposed to be your lifetime partner. God is love and since we have God dwelling on the inside, we give the love He has given us to others. That's when two spirits rejoice for coming to together and praise God for being made whole again.

Given by God; Written by;

Corrine Hooks

Is Love Easy?

Is Love easy? No, love is not always easy. It may look easy sometimes, but true love; true unconditional love is hard work. You have to work hard at loving others. The one you love may have some qualities that you may not always agree with but the spirit in them pushes pass the qualities that don't agree. One way to conquer them is to pray day and night for the things that are not of God to be delivered from that loved one so that the spirit in one another may continuously be in harmony. Sometimes it is best not to say a word when you are not in agreement. In the time when you are silent, fast and pray for clear understanding and clear communication with God.

Say this prayer with me: Heavenly and gracious Father, we come humbly asking you first to forgive us of everything we have done that was not like you, and we ask that you will open up our understanding of what you want us to do for you today regarding the ones we love, Lord help us to be obedient to every word you command of us, we know that the spirit man is willing but our flesh is weak, Lord we ask that you touch every area of our loved ones lives that they may see and obey you, Lord we thank you for supplying all our needs according to your riches in glory; Lord we praise you, glorify and magnify your Holy name , In Jesus name we pray, Amen.

Given by God; Written by:

Corrine Hooks

Prayer

Prayer, why do I pray; how do I pray; what and who should I pray for? These are all questions that I ask myself from time to time. God's word says that men (men & women) should always pray and never faint. Sometimes it is difficult to know what to pray for, but if you open up your heart and listen to God, He will give you a specific prayer for that moment. I often pray for others, which is the right thing to do, but sometimes we have to pray for ourselves. Pray for us to be renewed and strengthened in God; to grow into a new dimension in God; for clear understanding and direction of the purpose God has for our lives. When you are praying and you can't find words to say just stay on your knees and listen to what God has to and is saying to you. If you have questions trust and believe God will give you an answer to every question, concern, and every thought that crosses your mind. There is a song that says "Prayer will make it alright, Pray in and out of season, Pray when there's no special reason, don't be set in your ways just get on your knees and pray." That is all I can do when things seem to be out of control. When all else fails JUST PRAY!!!!!
Given by God; Written by:
Corrine Hooks

Marriage

Marriage is about compromise. It is not self-serving or overbearing. It is about covering each other in good times and in bad. It is about sacrifice; giving up your own wants to help supply the needs of your loved one. Marriage is about honoring your husband by not disrespecting him when he makes little or no money. It is about praying for one another at all times. It's about fasting together, caring for one another even when it is difficult, about walking away when you want to do something you may regret later. It's about never forgetting what you saw in each other when you first committed to those vows before God. It's remembering that God is first and wife/husband second, family third, and everything else is last. Marriage is about treating each other like king's and queen's, because we are apart of a royal priesthood (Galatians 4:7).

Say this prayer: Heavenly and gracious Father, we come humbly before you asking you to forgive us of our sins. Lord help us to follow you in this marriage the way you want us to go. Open up our understanding of each other and to never lose sight of You. Help us to remember who brought us together and who is holding this relationship in one piece. In Jesus name we pray. AMEN!

Given by God; Written by: Corrine Hooks

Used & Abused

When you feel spitefully, deliberately, and blatantly used and abused by someone, it hurts. It hurts the natural man and the spiritual man. The natural side of you says that you want to do something to hurt them back, but the spiritual side of you knows that you must pray for them. One thing we must do before we make any decisions in our lives we must first consult God. God said "In all your ways acknowledge me and I will direct your path" (Proverbs 3:6). We have to allow God to lead and guide our every decision even if it is something we really don't want to hear. It is to keep us from falling into something that could hurt us even more in the long run and then again it may not be the time that God has released you to do what you are asking His permission for. We are to listen and obey at all times. It is not for us to please the flesh but to please God. That is the only way we can make it into heaven.

Given by God; written by Corrine Hooks

True Worship

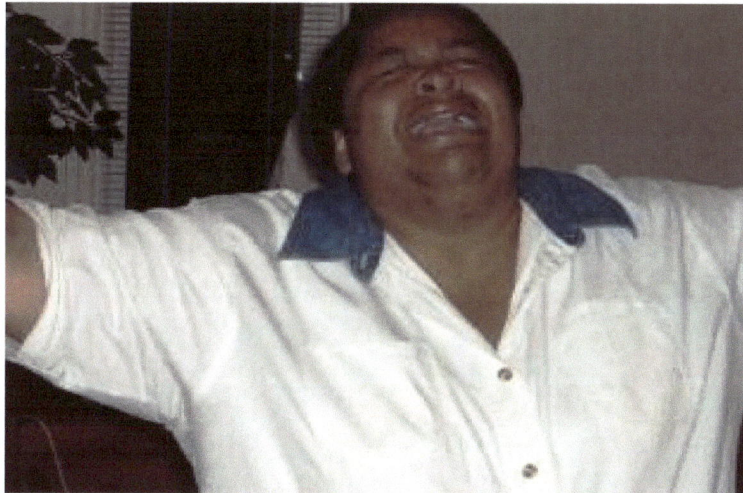

God loves us so much and all He requires is that we give Him our praise. But if you really want to get close to God, so close that you are nearly in His face give Him your true worship. True worship comes from a pure heart. You really love God with all your heart and soul. True worship doesn't just happen at church. True worship will happen any- and everywhere. It is a continuous praise spilling out of the heart and soul of those who love God. Sometimes it will feel like there are not enough words to express how you feel about God. The dictionary doesn't contain enough words to explain how awesome, glorious, magnificent, majestic, excellent, supreme, gracious, merciful, kind, loving, great, wonderful, beautiful, Holy, and forgiving God is.

Given By: God; Written By:

Corrine Hooks

Forgiveness

We are to forgive those who hurt us and we are to ask forgiveness of those we hurt. Jesus even asked God to forgive. "Jesus words were 'Father forgive them for they know not what they do'"(Luke 23:34 NIV). Flesh or the natural man doesn't always want to forgive, but in order to make it into heaven we have to ask for forgiveness of our sins daily and to forgive those who use and misuse us. Not only are we to forgive, we still have to love them as well. Love and forgive without an attitude because God does things for people who obey and obey with a cheerful heart. It makes things hard when you have an attitude about doing what God told you to do. And He really does not have to bless you, let alone allow you to live. So forgive and accept forgiveness.

Given by God; Written by:
Corrine Hooks

Quality

Time spent on our knees praying, reading the word of God, attending church, ministering to others, serving in areas of your church ministry are all ways of showing God quality time. It is also a way of showing God how much we love Him and glorify Him. Giving God all praise, honor and glory demonstrates the quality He has placed in us. God may call or wake you up at anytime to spend quality time with you. There are times when all you can do is praise Him, then there are times when you can only just listen for His instructions. The times you feel like weeping; it is best to weep yourself into a praise. Sooner or later you will stop weeping and a smile will rise on your face. Give God as much quality time as you give everything else in your life only extend His a lot more.

Given by: God

Written by: Corrine Hooks

To Be Used By God

To be used by God is a humbling and rewarding experience that we all should treasure. We are here on earth to promote God in everyway possible. To be used by God we have to be willing and obedient, have an open heart, and in constant prayer. It may seem easy but there is a process that must take place within us. We are not worthy to be used by God, which makes it even more lifting to know that He wants to use us. Being used by God we are going to endure some tests and trials. But that is to give us experience so that when we witness to the ones He has designated for our lives we know what we are talking about. When we endure those tests we receive a greater reward that no man can measure, because it can only come from God. Get to know Him so that He can use you for His glory and honor.

Given by God; Written By:
Corrine Hooks

Faith

Now Faith is the substance of things hope for and the evidence of things not seen (Hebrews 11:1). How much faith do you have? God's word says that if we have faith the size of a grain of a mustard seed (Luke 17:6) But without faith it is impossible to please God (Hebrews 11:6). Is your faith only at work when a love one is sick and you are believing God for their healing, or does your faith exceed when you want a new car or house? Our faith should always grow with each passing day. God is able to do exceedingly abundant above all that we can ask or think according to the power that works within us (Ephesians 3:20). So don't place God in a box by limiting your faith with little things. Let it explode to believe what you think is the impossible. And if we are just we are to live by faith (Galatians 3:11)

Given By God;

Written By: Corrine Hooks

Beauty

People have said that beauty is in the eye of the beholder but not everyone thinks that. Take me for instance; it took me a very long time to realize that I am a beautiful woman. The reason why is because others talked about me and made me feel self conscience about my body, name, clothes, and anything else they could think of. But you know what happened one day; I met someone by the name of God and His son Jesus. And I learned that they love me so much that He created me in His image and brought me into this world to be used by Him.

So ladies and gentlemen just remember God's words: "I am fearfully and wonderfully made (Psalm 139:14); "I know the thoughts I think toward you thoughts of good and not evil to bring you to an expected end" (Jeremiah 29:11); "You did not choose me, but I chose you and appointed you to go and bear fruit—fruit that will last" (John 15:16); and finally "I can do all things through Christ which strengthens me"
(Philippians 4:13).

Think differently, look differently, and carry yourself differently.
Be positive!!!!
Given By God; Written By: Corrine Hooks

Safe In His Arms

Have you ever felt like being held by a loved one, so much that you feel safe in their arms? Sometimes we don't have the luxury of having someone to hold us like that all the time. The only one who we know for sure that can hold us safe in His arms is God. He will hold you till all the hurt and pain you feel is gone from you, till you think that you have no more tears to cry, till you no longer feel the desire to give up on everything. It's not so much that we are depressed or housing one of the other negative feelings; it is just we as human beings get overwhelmed with the cares of this life and when that happens, we forget that God has us in His hands when we want to fall away into the comfortable, familiar arms of someone that has once had us feel that nothing can harm us. But we must realize that God is one who will never leave us or forsake us. It's in His word and His word can not come back to Him void (Isaiah 55:11). If you don't remember anything else, remember this: God is right there to hold you safely in His arms whenever, wherever, and however you need Him to.

Given by God; Written by:

Corrine Hooks

Teach Me

So many people say that it takes a village to raise a child. But God's word says "train up a child in the way he should go, and when he is old he will not depart from it" (Proverbs 22:6). Children are impressible and love to discover new things. A child may not always tell you they want to learn, but teach them something new and they are ready to run and tell the world what they have learned. We have to teach our children the old school way; values (manners, respect, honesty, sharing, caring, responsibility, and accountability). So teach, teach your children, other children, all children everything they will need to know, especially about God and who He is in your life, in order to make it in this present world.

Given by God; Written by:

Corrine Hooks

Strong Black Virtuous Woman

Proverbs 31 talks about a virtuous woman. Who can find a strong black virtuous woman? I have seen her. She is the first lady of my church, my grandmother, my church mother, mother, sisters, cousins, co-workers , friends, & every woman I have had the pleasure of meeting. A strong black woman doesn't make the choice to be a single mom but takes on the roll whenever necessary. A strong black virtuous woman covers her husband and family as well as makes sure that whatever/wherever help is needed she is there. Every black woman may not be strong. But she can become strong with God on her side. She can even become a virtuous woman by doing as God commanded and created her to do and be. If you want to learn how to become a virtuous woman read proverbs 31 and if you are a black woman that wants to become strong and virtuous then follow God, Christ and most of all your heart. Because if God dwells in the heart you can guarantee He is the one leading the way .

Given By God; Written by Corrine Hooks

My Unborn Seed

God has blessed me to conceive. He has blessed me with a seed. A seed that will grow naturally, spiritually, emotionally, and financially with the help and guidance of me and his father. God who is guiding us gives us the ability to nurture and cultivate our child into something awesome in His eyesight. Our seed has a great destiny that only God can provide. It is up to his/her father and mother to ensure that they train him/her up in the way of God so that when he/she is older they will not depart from Him. In doing this I must first place the seed in God's hands by dedicating them back to Him, reading the word and praying over them, protecting them everyway I can, putting away for the future, and loving them with the same unconditional love God has placed in me. If I fail at doing these things my seed will see destruction and Mayhem on every corner. No matter which way he or she turns there will be nothing but trouble for him/her. God has given me the power to care for our seed and that is what I plan to do.

Given by God; Written by: Corrine Hooks

Strong Black Man Of Valor

God has made man. But the black man has been created to be a man of valor. A black man has pride in himself and everything he does. A strong black man stands up for what he believes in and very seldom backs down from a challenge. A strong black man of valor follows Jesus' example. It may be a struggle for them in the beginning, but when he has been tried and tested several times, he learns to overcome other obstacles. A black man lead by God cares for his family like he cares for himself and most times more than himself. A strong black man of valor won't settle for less and won't give up on the promises of God. Men of God continue to lead by Jesus' example because somewhere another young man or boy is watching.

Given by God;

Written by: Corrine Hooks

Thousands of Thoughts

A thousand thoughts run through my mind. Is this real, is he telling me the truth or are there countless other girls just like you? If I tell him how I really feel he may lash out and will not see Christ in me, I will block the blessing God has in store for me and I will surely have to repent. But if I just keep silent and pray to God; tell Him everything I feel and want; no one will ever know the damage I would have caused. Because God is faithful and just to forgive me and will not throw it back in my face, the words I might have said out of anger. God's word says be angry and sin not. So I can be angry with whoever hurts me but I better take it to Jesus, for He will see me through. If these thoughts should ever rise again or if you should want to tell him off, ask God to help you so that you don't lose the testimony and race you have begun.

Given By: God

Written by: Corrine Hooks

A Woman Loves

How can a woman love a man that she just met, but feels she has known him all her life? How can a man speak words that not only arouses a woman's intellect but intimately as well? How can two people come together as one if God is not in it? Someone please explain this to me. There is a man that I love; I don't put him above God, because that would make him an idol and God said in His word there shall be no other god above me. But I do love this man. Sometimes it's hard to explain, you lose your breath when he whispers in your ear; you feel safe in his arms; you can't go a day without hearing his voice; you long to feel his touch but you know you can't give in to fast; you can't eat; you can't sleep. All you want is him. Who is this man you ask? If I told you; you wouldn't believe me.

Given by God;

Written By: Corrine Hooks

Lord, Why Me?

Lord, why did You consider me worthy enough for the tests I just faced? Were you trying me like Job? Lord I desire to understand why they chose to treat me that way and do the things they did to me and my family! God please help me to refocus my attention where You would have me to be, to do what You want me to do, to praise You inspite of the tests and trials I have faced. God you said in all thy getting get an understanding (Proverbs 4:7) and that is all I desire to have pertaining to these situations. God I am hurting, not physically but emotionally and I need Your help to pull me through. God I won't let You go until You bless my soul. Dear heavenly and gracious Father, I come asking You first to please forgive me for all my sins, those known and unknown, God I ask that You send Your deliverance and healing to me and others who face the hurt of loved ones causing them pain. In Jesus name I pray Amen!

Given By God; Written by Corrine Hooks

God's Will

To be in God's will is the only thing that I want. Not in my way, but His way is the best method to go. God will never steer you down a path that will ultimately destroy you. He will give you people and situations that will test your faith and trust in Him. It is to see if you will continue to believe with all your might or are you going to allow doubt to take over. God desires for us to obey every command that is in His word and given in His conversations (prayer) with us. We often ignore it to satisfy our flesh and in the long run we have to pay for it. Give thanks unto the Lord for His mercy endures forever. He said in His word that it is His will that we prosper and be in good health.
Get in God's Will!

Given by God;
Written by: Corrine Hooks

Set Free

God has released me from the bonds of captivity from the prison of my mind, and the hurt of my past & present. Whom the Son set free is truly free indeed (John 8:36). Freedom is a blessing and a wonderful feeling. When we understand that Jesus came not only to save but to set us free because He & The Father truly love us we will be able to walk in the newness of life. A person that is free in the Father, Son, and Holy Spirit has peace of mind, joy, patience, is faithful, kind, gentle, has goodness and self-control (Galatians 5:22). I'm no longer trapped by the snares the enemy set for me (II Timothy 2:26).

Heavenly, gracious & merciful Father I give you thanksgiving and praise first for loving me so much that you sent your Son as a ransom for me and allowing Him to set me free from bondage; Secondly I honor You for all Your many wonderful blessings and favor you give to me daily. I love You with all my heart & soul. In Jesus name Amen!

Given by God
Written by: Corrine Hooks

Longing

I longed to be held by my father and loved by my mother. I longed to see my mother's mother and get to know my father's mother. I longed to meet and greet the aunts I never knew. But the One who has filled all those longings was God. He came along and made sure the voids I felt in life were filled with love (Romans 5:8), purpose (Isaiah 30:2, Romans 8:28), understanding (Philippians 4:6-7), patience (Psalm 37:7-9), and strength (Psalm 138:3, Isaiah 40:31).

So now I no longer have a longing. I have been made complete because I am part of a royal priesthood (I Peter 2:9) and I am the righteousness of God (II Corinthians 5:21).

Given by: God
Written by: Corrine Hooks

Promises

If a man/woman makes a promise they can or may not keep it. But when God makes a promise you can best believe He will do it. God's promises are found all throughout His Holy word (the bible). Some of those promises are eternal life (John 10:28), salvation (Hebrews 6), good health (Jeremiah 30:17), prosperity (III John 1:2), love (Romans 5:8), faith (Hebrews 11:32-40), peace (Isaiah 26:3), healing (Malachi 4:2), joy (Psalm 30:5), protection (Psalm 91:10), favor (Psalm 119:58), and grace (Romans 4:16). He has more but you have to read His word to find out what they are. Remember the next time a woman or man makes a promise doesn't guarantee that it will be kept. But God is not a man that He would lie nor the Son of Man that He would repent (Numbers 23:19). His word will not return to Him void but will accomplish all that He has sent it forth to do (Isaiah 55:11). God is just in keeping His promises (II Peter 3:9).

Given by: God
Written by: Corrine Hooks

www.ingramcontent.com/pod-product-compliance
Lightning Source LLC
Chambersburg PA
CBHW041239040426

42445CB00004B/89